Performance Management

90 Minute Guides

Michelle N. Halsey

Silver City Publications & Training, L.L.C.
P.O. Box 1914
Nampa, ID 83653
https://www.silvercitypublications.com/shop/

ISBN-10: 1-64004-032-3
ISBN-13: 978-1-64004-032-8

Contents

Chapter 1 – The Basics

Performance Management is not a company's way of employing "micro-managing" techniques that stunt the professional growth of its employees. But rather, it is a strategic approach to ensuring the efficiency and effectiveness of an organization. Whether at the organizational, departmental or employee level, the goal of performance management is to make sure all business goals are being met in a satisfactorily manner.

By the end of this chapter, you will be able to:

- Define performance management.

- Understand how performance management works and the tools to make it work.

- Learn the three phases of performance management and how to assess it.

- Discuss effective goal-setting.

- Learn how to give feedback on performance management.

- Identify Kolb's Learning Cycle.

- Recognize the importance of motivation.

- Develop a performance journal and performance plan.

The Basics

The effectiveness of an organization in terms of whether or not it is meeting its mission or goals can be determined by engaging in performance management. According to the U.S. Office of Personnel Management, performance management consists of five components: "Planning work and setting expectations, continually monitoring performance, developing the capacity to perform, periodically rating performance in a summary fashion, and rewarding."

What is Performance Management?

The phrase "Performance Management" was coined in the 1970s by Dr. Aubrey Daniels, a clinical psychologist. At the time, he used it to describe technology and the importance of managing behavior and the result of the behavior. Effective management would ensure proper behaviors are being executed, which would in turn produce favorable results. He later associated this approach to the interactions of people whether in a formal or informal setting.

With the proper training, management can manipulate the conditions of the workplace (e.g. policies and procedures, available skills to train and motivate employees) in order to measure the true success of the business – that is the financial standing of a company as well as the individual success of its employees.

How Does Performance Management Work?

The drive to implement a performance management system is not sufficient. Management as well as employees must put forth the effort necessary to make it happen. With "all hands on deck" and the observation of the following, organizations can build a successful program.

- Clearly identify the job's purpose as well as the duties associated with it.

- Determine goals and how to measure outcomes.

- Rank job priority.

- Characterize the standard of performance for critical aspects of the position.

- Discuss employee performance and provide feedback. This should at least be done on a quarterly basis.

- Keep track of performance records.

- If necessary, create an improvement plan to better employees' performance.

Tools

It is unrealistic to expect employees to perform at an optimal level without providing them with the tools to succeed. The following tools are crucial to the achievement of the system.

Model of standards: Creating a model that clearly defines employee performance standards helps the company and employees avoid ambiguities in what is expected. It also enables employers to provide their employees with specific feedback, which is greatly beneficial because it potentially increases job satisfaction.

Whether in writing or delivered verbally, performance standards are enforceable. It is, however advisable that they are captured in writing to avoid questions in the future.

There should be a set standard for every aspect of one's position. For example, an employee who is a Customer Service/Sales Representative may be expected to take and sufficiently answer the service questions of 10 customers an hour. This employee may also be required to upsell products to 50% of the clients he talks to.

There are several factors to keep in mind when developing this model. Performance standards should:

- Be realistic in terms of whether or not it can be attained as well as whether or not employees have adequate training.

- Be measurable with regard to quantity, quality, time, etc.

- Be clear in defining the proper method for gathering performance information and how it measures against the standard.

Annual Employee Appraisal Document: While employers monitor employees' performance throughout the year and provide feedback and coaching during that interval, employers are also responsible for conducting an employee appraisal, which is generally done on an annual basis. The appraisal allows the employer to summarize the employee's performance, gauge job satisfaction, as well as prepare for the future.

Coaching: Once the standard has been set and performance feedback has been provided to the employee, it is critical that the employer offer some type of coaching. The purpose of coaching is to strengthen areas of improvement as well as enhance areas where the employee is currently successful. In order to accomplish this, coaching must be done in a positive manner. The words used must build and not destroy. Diplomacy is important when providing coaching. Coaching promotes employee motivation as well as continued success.

A Performance Management system is only as good as its evaluation process. It is not enough to implement an effective program that covers all the basics, but you must be able to measure its success via assessments and performance reviews. This will in turn allow you to see where modifications need to take place (e.g. in the performance management system itself, performance of the company as a whole or specific employee performance).

Three Phase Process

Kurt Lewin, also known as the "founder of social psychology", introduced a three-phase theory of change that goes hand-in-hand with performance management. The process includes the following:

Phase One: Unfreezing: This phase is extremely important as you aim to understand change and how it takes place. This phase is crucial because it includes coming to the realization that change needs to happen. It also requires one to leave that which has been comfortable in order to make this change possible.

In order for someone to decide whether or not they are willing to change, they must weigh the advantages and disadvantages of this being done. This concept is what Force Field Analysis is based on. Force Field Analysis considers the different factors that work for and against the change that one must understand in order to make a decision.

Phase Two: Change: In Lewin's model, he pointed out that "change" is not a one-time event that takes place, but rather the inner-transition that takes place as a response to the outward changes that are taking place.

Due to the uncertainties of "what will happen next", this phase is considered one of the more difficult ones to achieve. And because of this, it is important for employees to have access to training and coaching to help ease the transition.

Phase Three: Freezing: Also known as "refreezing", this phase is the establishment of new norms and gaining stability after the institution of change. This phase can sometimes be misleading. It seems to be a long-term state, when in fact it is one that can change to "Unfreezing" within a matter of days. So, although this stage cannot be viewed as the "last", having the ability to successfully make it to this point is a great accomplishment. This could allude to the fact that it is becoming easier for someone to adjust to change, which is crucial because it happens regularly.

Assessments

There are a variety of assessments that can be utilized to determine skill, knowledge, and ability. These assessments can be administered when the individual is a prospective employee or an actual employee.

Types of Assessments

Pre-Screening: A Pre-Screening Assessment can be used to find out information on a prospective employees skills and knowledge before committing to hire them and this can save the employer costly mistakes down the road.

360-Degree Review: As its name implies, this type of assessment takes a comprehensive look at an employee with regard to their work performance. This information can be attained by involving a diverse pool of individuals, with varying levels of interaction with the employee (e.g. supervisor, peers, clients, etc.)

Knowledge: This type of assessment generally takes on a questionnaire format. It allows the employer to ask specific questions on topics relating to the business, usually in the form of multiple choice questions.

Performance Reviews

According to Entrepreneur.com, a performance review is defined as "An analysis of an employee's work habits undertaken at a fixed point in time to determine the degree to which stated objectives and expectations have been reached."

While each company has its own ideas of what a performance review should include, here are steps that should be taken with regard to all performance reviews:

- **Preparation:** Both the employer and employee must be adequately groomed for the review. This may involve reviewing any notes, engaging in a one-on-one discussion with the employee beforehand or simply making the employee aware of the review in advance.

- **Prioritize the meeting:** To show the employee that this review is a top priority, there should be a formal agenda that is adhered to. There should also be as few interruptions as possible.

- **Encourage positivity:** When speaking to the employee, invoke positive responses by communicating in a positive manner.

- **Clarity:** Be sure the purpose of the meeting is clear from the beginning.

- **Expectations:** Review the job description, why it is needed, and the standards of performance.

- **Explain employee's performance:** Discuss the employee's actual performance, whether it fell below, met or exceeded expectations. Give specific examples.

- **Employee feedback:** Allow the employee to express their concerns or suggestions.

- **Goal-setting**: Discuss goals for areas that require improvement. If there are no "areas for improvement", create goals to enhance the knowledge and skills of the employee for personal development as well as bettering the department / company as a whole.

- **Follow-up:** Determine the appropriate method and or time for follow-up.

- **Closing:** The meeting should end positively. Review the contributions the employee is making to the company. Inform employee that you are willing to help in any way necessary.

Chapter 2 – Goal Setting

Every successful business plan requires goals and objectives. Goals show the strengths and weaknesses of plans and procedures. Implementing regularly evaluated goals allows leaders to understand where performance is and what needs to be improved. When managing performance, make sure that you implement SMART goals.

SMART Goal Setting

People often fail to reach their goals. This usually indicates that the wrong goals are being chosen. SMART goals will improve the chances of achieving both personal and business goals.

SMART goals:

- **Specific:** Goals should have specific instructions.

- **Measurable:** It should be clear when goals and objectives are met.

- **Attainable:** Impossible goals are not motivating.

- **Realistic:** Goals need to be something people are able to work towards.

- **Timely:** Goals need specific timeframes.

Specific Goals

Goals need to be specific. Employees need to understand exactly what they are expected to do. It is not enough to simply ask for improvement. This is a general goal. Specific goals explain who is involved and what goal should be achieved. It can also identify a location, requirements, and reasoning behind the goal.

Example:

- **General goal:** Improve performance.

- **Specific goal**: Meet with your mentor once a week.

Measurable Goals

Goals need to be measurable in order to be effective. They specify how much or how many. Measurable goals allow employees to identify when they have accomplished their goals.

Example:

- **General goal**: Increase sales.

- **Measurable goal**: Increase sales 7 percent over last year's.

Attainable Goals

Goals must always be attainable. Employees need goals that challenge them but must still be within reach. When goals are seen as unattainable, employees will give up on them without even trying. The measure of a goal should always be within reach.

- **Unattainable goal**: Reduce turnover by 60 percent.

- **Attainable goal:** Reduce turnover by 10 percent.

Realistic Goals

Employees need realistic goals. It is important that employees are able to achieve their goals. The goals need to relate directly to employee abilities, and it is important to make sure that they have the tools necessary to meet them. Breaking larger goals down to smaller achievements will make them more realistic.

Example:

- **Realistic Goal:** The production department currently makes 200 cars a week. With new training, they will create 225 a week.

Timely Goals

Goals should always have a time frame. General goals do not establish a time frame. Time frames encourage employees to move forward. Having specific dates will also determine when goals are reevaluated.

Example:

- **General goal**: Increase sales.

- **Timely goal**: Increase sales within six months.

Monitoring Results

Once goals are established, it is important to monitor their results. This will determine how effective a plan or strategy is. Use a basic evaluation to determine what changes need to be made in a plan and reevaluate your goals.

What to evaluate:

- Were the goals and objectives achieved?

- Were they achieved in the established time frame?

- What is the feedback from employees and leadership?

- What are the financial gains or losses?

Chapter 3 – Establishing Performance Goals

Performance goals require strategic action. To be effective, these goals should not be handed down to employees. It is important to include employees in the goal setting process and encourage them to meet their individual performance goals. This will improve individual and company performance.

Strategic Planning

A strategic plan determines where employees are, where they want to be, and how they will get there. It should embrace the values of the organization and align with the following company information. The organization must create a strategic plan before creating performance goals.

Company Strategic Plan:

- Vision

- Mission

- Philosophy

- Goals

- Objectives

Employee performance goals need to consider the company's strategic plan. Individual performance goals must be SMART goals that include strategies and actions for employees to take.

Example Goal: Stay informed about innovations in the industry, it can help improve productivity by 10 percent this year.

Examples of Actions:

- Attend training classes

- Meet with a mentor

- Communicate consistently

Job Analysis

A job analysis determines what is required to do a specific job. It will help determine which skills and attributes an employee needs to complete a job successfully. A job analysis will help determine who to hire, how to train, and what compensation a job should receive. Job analyses are instrumental in determining performance. Research a position to determine the following information:

Job Requirements:

- Responsibilities

- Tools or systems used

- Reporting requirements

Employee Requirements:

- Training/Education

- Skills

- Aptitudes

- Necessary certification

Setting Goals

Performance goals need to be SMART goals. They need to address behavior, competency, and results. Remember to involve employees in their performance goals.

Examples of Goals:

- **Behavior**: Employees have complained about distance. Communicate with employees in person every week, rather than just sending emails.

- **Competency:** New equipment is being installed. Perform all the training within three weeks.

- **Results:** Sales are down. Increase sales by 5 percent this quarter.

Motivation

Performance is related to motivation. Motivation is the job of every leader. There is not a single method for motivating employees. People have different personal motives, and leaders must meet the needs of individuals.

Motivating Tips:

- **Lead by example**: Motivate yourself before you can motivate others.

- **Meet with individuals**: Communicate with employees directly to find out what motivates them.

- **Reward employees**: Find motivating rewards for individuals.

- **Delegate**: Do not micromanage employees.

- **Inform**: Inform people about how they are making a difference in the organization.

- **Celebrate**: Pay attention to achievements and celebrate with employees.

Chapter 4 – 360 Degree Feedback

360 degree feedback is useful for evaluating performance. It provides evaluations from different sources to paint a clear picture of how well an individual performs. Identifying strengths and weaknesses will allow employees to continually improve how they perform.

What is 360 Degree Feedback?

360 degree feedback is an alternative method of reviewing employees. Rather than a traditional review, employees are given anonymous feedback from supervisors and peers. Managers' feedback also includes direct reports and reviews from employees. Individuals also evaluate themselves in 360 degree feedback. Together, these evaluations will help improve performance by:

- Identifying and enhancing strengths

- Identifying areas that need development

- Helping Employees set goals

- Creating action plans

Vs. Traditional Performance Reviews

360 degree feedback provides a better picture of performance than traditional reviews. Supervisors perform traditional performance reviews. Traditional review can have a negative impact on performance, if employees feel it is not fair. This can damage trust between managers and employees. Traditional performance reviews also do little to encourage cooperation between employees because coworkers do not influence scores on traditional reviews. People in positions of authority also benefit from 360 degree feedback. Traditional performance reviews do not always give an accurate description of employer/employee relationships.

The Components

360 degree feedback evaluation forms are typically done on a scale of 1 to 10. There is a place for comments on the evaluation form. The scores from supervisors, peers, employees, and direct reports are averaged and compared with average company scores. HR typically

handles the reporting to make sure that the feedback remains confidential.

Example:

Computer Skills

1_____2_____3_____4_____5_____

Comments:

_____

Chapter 5 – Competency Assessments

Competency assessments are essential to performance management. These assessments make it easier to hire and promote the right people. They also help assess performance and the different competencies that employees need to improve. It will also identify the top performers.

Competency Assessment Defined

Competencies are a set of skills and essential knowledge that are necessary to perform a job well. The competencies for every position should be defined before hiring. They are important to the hiring and guide the interview process. A competency assessment assesses the skills of employees and compares them with previously established core competencies. A supervisor or HR professional decides the score of each assessment. The performance is based on chosen indicators and separate level for each rating. Each company has its own competency assessment levels, but most assessments include the following ratings:

Sample Rating:

- Excellent

- Meets expectations

- Needs improvement

- Not applicable

- Have opportunities to advance

Implementation

There are several steps that you need to take before you implement competency assessments. Successful implementation requires you to complete all of the steps.

Steps:

- **Identify Competencies**: Ascertain which competencies are needed to perform a job and the skill level of each competency.

- **Develop Assessments**: Create a fair method of assessment that concentrates on targets. Company goals will determine the targets.

- **Practice Assessments**: Practice using assessments, just like any other skill.

- **Assess Employees**: Use the standards and assessments to review employees.

- **Plan**: Use action plans to help employees develop.

Final Destination

The final destination will provide a pool of trained professionals with strong performance. Each company will have its own final destination that depends on the goals and needs. Reaching the stage of final destination may mean completely overhauling the competency program. It could also mean placing more attention on action plans and training. It all depends on the competencies required for each role. Identifying the goals of the organization and the competencies of each position will allow your organization to reach the final destination.

Chapter 6 – Kolb's Learning Cycle

Kolb's Learning Cycle states that learning is based on experience. The learning cycle has four basic elements: experience, observation, conceptualization, and experimentation. It is important to be familiar with the learning cycle to effectively manage performance, and guide employees to greater achievements.

Experience

Kolb describes the importance of concrete experience. Concrete experience is direct experience that involves the senses. It is not simply knowledge about a subject. Hands-on training is an example of concrete experience that employees learn at work. Experience and conceptualization are the two ways that employees take in knowledge.

Observation

Kolb defines observation as reflective observation. It is what the concrete experience means to the person learning. Watching is the way that knowledge is transformed into meaning for an individual. This is where the connotations are created as learners see different perspectives. An example would be watching a trainer perform a task again or considering a task recently performed. Experimentation is another way to transform knowledge.

Conceptualization

Abstract conceptualization is a way to gather knowledge on a subject without direct experience. This involves a basic understanding of a situation by applying logic. An example of this would be reading a training manual. Abstract conceptualization is having the knowledge about something.

Experimentation

Active experimentation is the final part of Kolb's Learning Cycle. Here, people learn by doing. They transform knowledge by acting on it. An example of this would be using a new computer program. Active experimentation involves taking risks based on the knowledge people have gathered. It is important that employees be allowed to take risks when learning.

Chapter 7 – Motivation

Every employee needs to be motivated in order for performance management to be successful. While employees must take some responsibility in motivating themselves, management can help motivate and develop individuals. Practicing basic motivational techniques will improve performance as it boosts morale.

Key Factors

Motivation is more than being satisfied. Motivation is what causes employees to go the extra mile and commit to a project or company. Fredrick Herzberg identified the key factors that drive motivation in employees across different fields. Pay and work conditions were tied to satisfaction. Poor pay and work conditions adversely affect productivity, but positive pay and work conditions do little to increase motivation.

Motivators:

- **Responsibility:** Employees should have a sense of ownership in their work.

- **Nature of the work:** The nature of the work can help motivate people.

- **Recognition:** Employee efforts need to be recognized.

- **Achievement:** People need to feel like they are achieving something worthwhile.

The Motivation Organization

People perform better when they believe in their company. When the values of an organization match the personal values of employees, an organization will be highly motivated. This is why socially responsible companies are able to easily attract talent. They speak to an individual's internal motivators. Businesses that address internal motivations are more likely to be high performing.

Internal Motivations:

- Family

- Environment

- Success

- Community

- Personal time

Identifying Personal Motivators

Each person has a different set of motivators. Some people respond better to verbal praise and others need rewards. It is important to motivate employees on a personal level. This is easier to do in small organizations. Large companies will have to rely on each manager to identify personal motivators.

Techniques to Identify Personal Motivators:

- Observation: Observe how individuals respond to different motivators and take notes.

- Communication: Get to know each employee, and identify personal motivators.

- Surveys: Have employees fill out surveys that identify what motivates them.

Evaluating and Adapting

Like everything else, it is essential to evaluate and adapt motivation techniques. This should include the following steps:

- Surveys: Surveys will show the level of engagement and how motivated employees are.

- Review mission: Compare the mission, policies, and procedures to internal motivators. Are they aligned?

- Development: Examine the number of employees who have advanced within the company.

- Goals: Whether or not company goals are met is an indication of motivation.

Adapt motivation techniques as necessary to improve performance and engage employees.

Chapter 8 – The Performance Journal

Performance journals create evaluations that are more accurate by allowing employees and manager to keep track of performance throughout the year. Both managers and employees can keep journals. This will help guide and develop employees who challenge themselves and improve performance.

Record Goals and Accomplishments

It is important to record your goals and accomplishments. Even minor accomplishments need to go in the performance journal. Seeing your accomplishments will encourage you, and seeing your goals will motivate you to continue working towards them. Comparing goals and accomplishments will help you focus on what you need to do to improve performance.

Employee Records:

- **Accomplishments:** Include recognitions and awards.

- **Challenges:** Include requests for training or other help to meet goals.

Employer Records:

- **Accomplishments:** Details include documentation and notes.

- **Evaluation:** Include performance gaps and direct reports.

Linking with Your Employees or Managers

It is important that employees and managers connect for performance management to be effective. Relationships on every level must remain professional. When employees and managers do not trust each other, performance suffers. It is possible for managers to link to employees' performance journals and see any information that employees choose to share with them. This helps managers see things from an employee's perspective and create accurate evaluations. It also makes employees part of the evaluation process.

Implementing a Performance Coach

A performance coach will help people meet their needs to improve performance. In most organizations, managers act as performance coaches. How well managers coach performance affects the quality of employee performance. Managers must communicate effectively with each employee and motivate that person to excel. This requires a combination of encouragement, praise, and correction. Assess and coach employees in the following areas.

Coaching Assessments:

- Assess skills and knowledge: Provide any necessary training.

- Assess the tools: Make sure that the individual has everything necessary to complete his or her job.

- Assess the processes: Improve procedures to help employees, or instruct them in using different procedures.

- Assess motivation: Motivate people on a personal level.

Keeping Track

Coaches need to keep track of employee progress. This will help them create strategies that will challenge employees and help them grow. There are several ways to keep track of performance.

- Traditional Evaluations

- 360 Feedback

- Journals

- Performance log

A performance log is where you can make notes of any observations regarding performance. This will help you become a better coach.

Chapter 9 – Creating a Performance Plan

A performance plan is essential to performance management. It is a strategic plan that each individual needs to follow to become high performing employees. Managers must create a plan with every employee they work with. There is always room for improvement.

Goals

Establish professional goals that reflect the needs of the organization and individual. Make sure that employees have the tools to reach these goals and provide them if they do not. This will improve productivity and performance.

Setting Goals:

- Determine what employees need to accomplish.

- Make SMART goals.

- Allow employees to develop the goals with you.

Example:

- Enroll in a speaking class within three months to facilitate meetings by the end of the year.

Desired Results

The results of a performance plan are not strategies. They are what employees are expected to achieve, and this should be made clear in the performance plan. Employees are responsible for achieving the desired results. For example, a desired result may be to consistently meet sales goals. The ability or inability to meet desired results determines the level of performance. An individual who cannot meet desired results will need coaching in that area.

Prioritization

It is important to prioritize goals. Employees should focus on the top three goals. The goals given priority need to align with the company goals and the top competencies of each position. These usually influence productivity and cost. A nonessential goal such as filing at the end of each day does not take priority. Make sure that goals do not conflict with each other.

Example of Prioritizing Goals:

- Train to use the new software within two months.

- Call clients every week to increase customer satisfaction.

- Meet monthly sales goals with social networking, cold calling, and scheduled meetings.

Measure

Performance must be measured. This is not always easy because some tasks may be subjective. There must be fair standards and measurement established for each position. You will need to consider the job requirements and employee competencies that you previously established. It is also helpful to make the measurements cost specific, when possible. Create a rating scale for each measure. It can be numbered or not.

Measurement Example:

- The total number of customer complaints.

- Percentage of wasted product.

- Met personal goals

Evaluation

Compare the measurements against performance to evaluate employees. It is also important to include whether or not employees achieved their goals and met desired expectations. This information is normally included in an employee evaluation form. Formal reviews are typically done every year, but frequent informal reviews are more effective. Meet with employees regularly to evaluate performance. Use the same criteria as a formal evaluation to help direct and improve performance.

Additional Titles

The 90 Minute Guide series of books covers a variety of general business skills and are intended to be completed in 90 minutes or less. It is an effective way for building your skill set and can be used to acquire professional development units needed by project managers and other industries to maintain their certification. For the availability of titles please see

https://www.silvercitypublications.com/shop/.

No. 1 - Appreciative Inquiry

No. 2 - Assertiveness and Self Control

No. 3 - Attention Management

No. 4 - Body Language Basics

No. 5 - Business Acumen

No. 6 - Business and Etiquette

No. 7 - Change Management

No. 8 - Coaching and Mentoring

No. 9 - Communications Strategies

No. 10 - Conflict Resolution

No. 11 - Creative Problem Solving

No. 12 - Delivering Constructive Criticism

No. 13 - Developing Creativity

No. 14 - Developing Emotional Intelligence

No. 15 - Developing Interpersonal Skills

No. 16 - Developing Social Intelligence

No. 17 - Employee Motivation

No. 18 - Facilitation Skills

No. 19 - Goal Setting and Getting Things Done

No. 20 - Knowledge Management Fundamentals

No. 21 - Leadership and Influence

No. 22 - Lean Process and Six Sigma Basics

No. 23 - Managing Anger

No. 24 - Meeting Management

No. 25 - Negotiation Skills

No. 26 - Networking Inside a Company

No. 27 - Networking Outside a Company

No. 28 - Office Politics for Managers

No. 29 - Organizational Skills

No. 30 - Performance Management

No. 31 - Presentation Skills

No. 32 - Public Speaking

No. 33 - Servant Leadership

www.ingramcontent.com/pod-product-compliance
Lightning Source LLC
Chambersburg PA
CBHW070723210326
41520CB00016B/4433